The
Young Letterer

The greatest example of classic Roman lettering: part of the inscription on the Trajan Column at Rome, cut about AD 113

The Young Letterer

A HOW-IT-IS-DONE BOOK OF LETTERING

by

Tony Hart

FREDERICK WARNE & CO., INC.
New York and London

TABLE OF CONTENTS

Library of Congress Catalog Card No. 66 – 13792

Copyright © 1965 by Nicholas Kaye Ltd
ALL RIGHTS RESERVED

Printed in Great Britain

INTRODUCTION

This is a book about lettering. But it is more than that, it's about writing and that is something we all have to do. Sometimes what we *say* in writing is the most important thing, as in books, letters, newspapers, notices, addresses and so on; and sometimes the writing itself is the most important part, as with a name over a shop, or the cover of a magazine or the name of your house. Mostly we try to make both the writing and the lettering important. This way we can achieve good design with what we want to say.

Really, what we are trying to do is to take the letter characters that have been passed on to us through the ages and put them down for people to read in the best ways that we know. In this book, I shall tell you something of how we came to have our letters and two ways in which we can write them down—one with the pen, which is an ancient craft, and one with the brush, another art form which we call 'drawn lettering'. And if any of my 'know-how' can serve to help *you* to know how to letter, too, then I shall be happy. You will find it a fascinating form of craftsmanship and everyone else will benefit from yet another good young letterer.

These are hieroglyphs. The ancient Egyptians' writing shows how they achieved good design with what they wanted to say. In the form shown here the picture writing reads 'Pharaoh'. From these pictures came—

and ultimately—

On this page you can see how pictures can come to represent letters in an alphabet, and an early alphabet made up of symbols we know well.

Some are slightly different to those of the alphabet we know and there aren't as many. The two large symbols we take for granted, but the figure 7 doesn't read as 'seven'—it is an Arabic symbol, like the originals of our other figures from 1 to 9. The ampersand is an abbreviation: we read 'and', but it is a monogram of the letters *et*, the Latin for *and*.

6

GOD 天 SUN 目 MOON 月 BRIGHT 朋

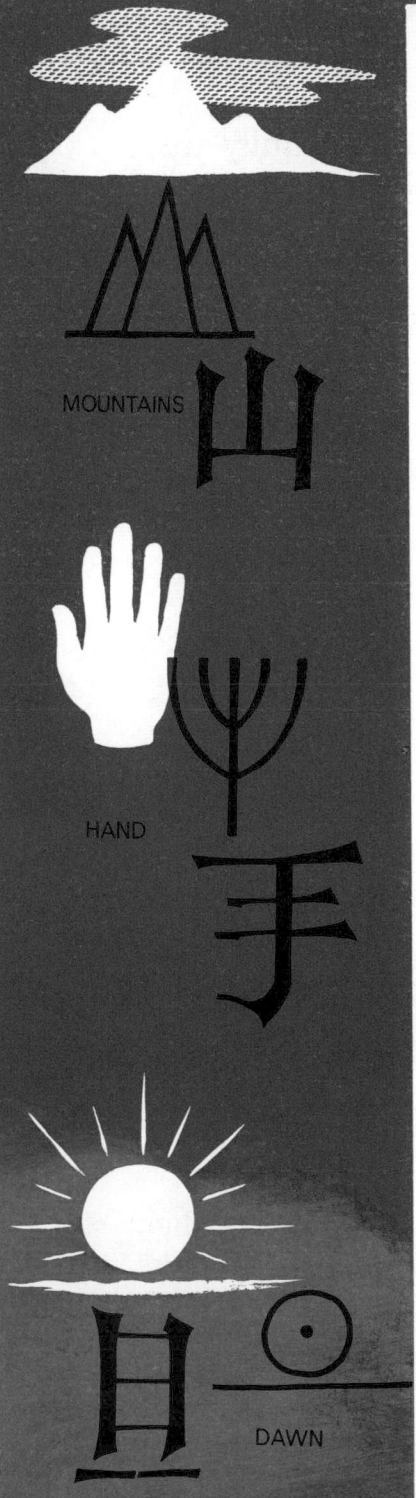

MOUNTAINS 山

HAND 手

DAWN 旦

WHAT IS LETTERING?

The earliest forms of communication by writing were pictures—the ancient Chinese made pictures representing what they wanted to put down. These *pictograms*, after constant use, became more stylized and finally became the characters that are used now. Two, or more, characters were often combined. For instance, the Chinese characters for 'sun' and 'moon' could be put together to form a single character meaning 'bright'.

The pictures on this page tell their own story, but the Chinese picture characters are not *letters*. The ancient Egyptians started out with pictograms (we call theirs *hieroglyphs*), but these actually turned into symbols representing sounds of speech (*phonograms*), so that they did become characters of the alphabet, or letters. Look at the hieroglyphs on the opposite page. You can see quite easily what some of the pictures mean: birds, snakes, feet walking and vases. The sounds the Egyptians used for such things were eventually used as the sounds for letters—so that 'a crocodile skin' sounded like E, 'an owl'—M and 'a cake'—T. The word made up of the letters EMT sounds like the Egyptian word for Egypt.

7

The *alphabet*, so called after the first two Greek letters, Alpha and Beta, derived from way back, some time in the ninth century B.C. We say now that it started as a *proto-Semitic* set of characters, but whether it came from Cyprus, Egypt, Babylon or Crete no one has yet proved. It's interesting, though, to know that in the Semitic etymology (which is the origin and study of words) the first two Hebrew letters are Aleph and Beth.

Today we find three important alphabets: *Latin, Arabic* and *Cyrillic*. Cyrillic is the Slav form as used in Russia. Arabic, as we have seen, has given us our numerals. But from now on it is the Latin alphabet we shall look at.

I have constructed a pruned version of the alphabet 'family tree'. Many twigs are missing, but the main branches are there all right.

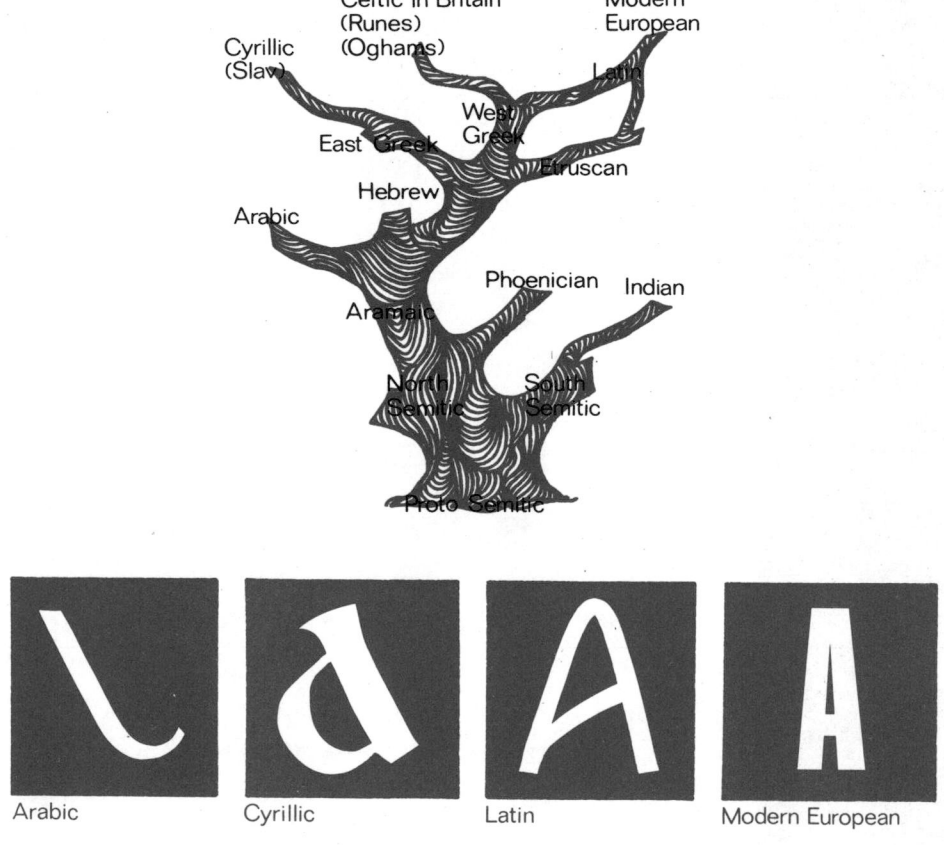

| Arabic | Cyrillic | Latin | Modern European |

And so we come to the symbols we all know and use every day. From here on, we are in the 'how-to-do-it' part—not only how to make the marks and what to make them with, but what to put them on. So let's have a look at materials.

8

MATERIALS

When I was an art student, I was taught how to stretch paper. This gives you a beautifully flat surface, one that will not wrinkle in use, and that is far cheaper than prepared board. With practice, you will find the technique easy. You need a small drawing-board, plenty of gummed strip and your paper. The best paper to use is a rag content drawing paper. I don't mean the most expensive kind, although later on you will wish to use beautiful paper for your beautiful lettering.

First, thoroughly soak the paper in water—let the surplus water drain off and lay the damp sheet on the drawing-board. For the next few minutes the paper will be expanding, so you won't stick it down until it's 'on the turn'. It contracts as it dries and you are going to hold it back with gummed strip so that it dries taut. When the paper is just damp to the touch, wet the gummed strip and stick down the sheet by framing it on all four sides. Undoubtedly the result will look untidy, the paper will probably have waves in it— never mind. Concentrate on getting the gummed strip flush to the paper and to the board. Let it dry away from any fierce heat—that will only hurry the process and something will crack! In an hour or so, you will have a sheet of paper taut as a drum to work on.

10

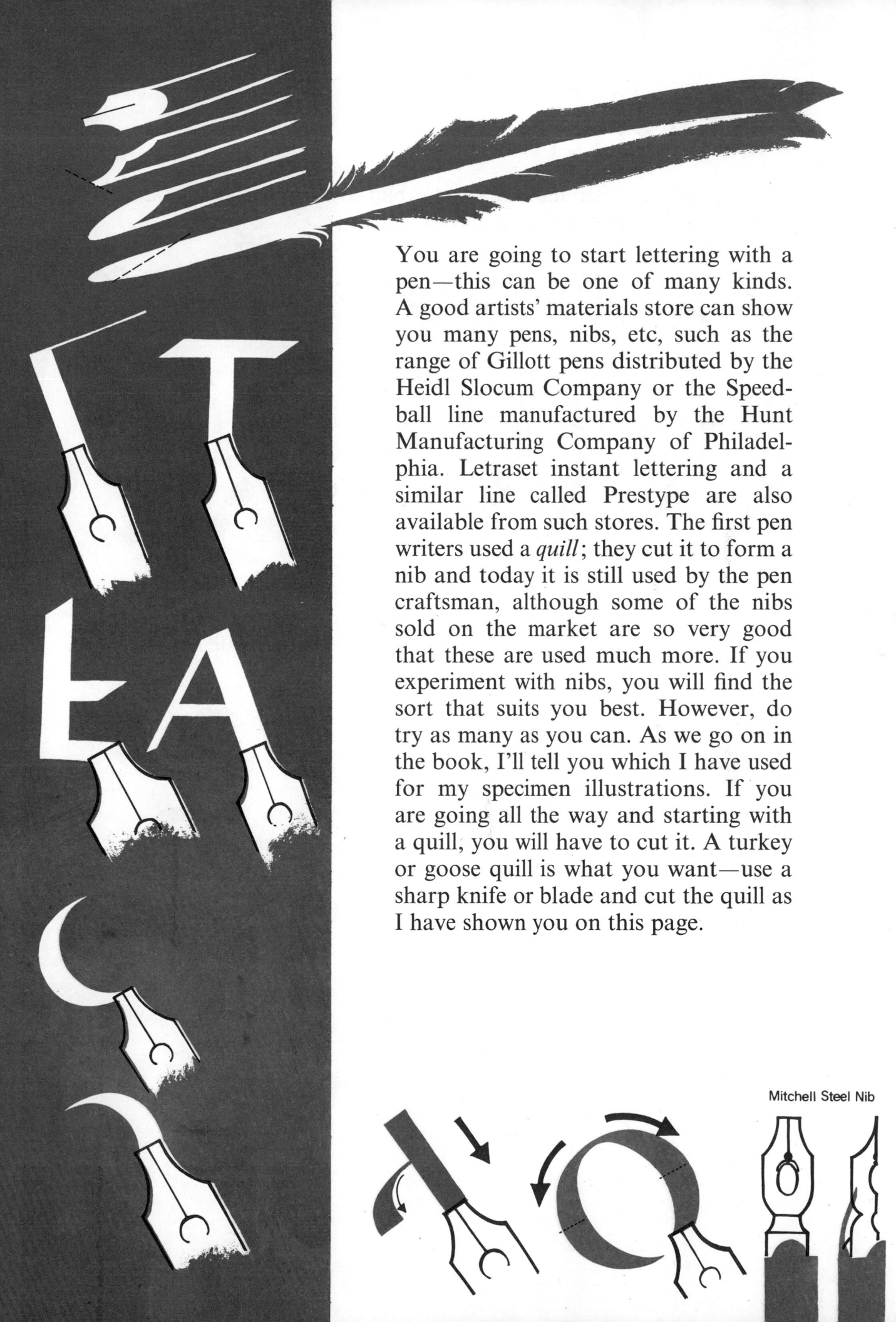

You are going to start lettering with a pen—this can be one of many kinds. A good artists' materials store can show you many pens, nibs, etc, such as the range of Gillott pens distributed by the Heidl Slocum Company or the Speedball line manufactured by the Hunt Manufacturing Company of Philadelphia. Letraset instant lettering and a similar line called Prestype are also available from such stores. The first pen writers used a *quill*; they cut it to form a nib and today it is still used by the pen craftsman, although some of the nibs sold on the market are so very good that these are used much more. If you experiment with nibs, you will find the sort that suits you best. However, do try as many as you can. As we go on in the book, I'll tell you which I have used for my specimen illustrations. If you are going all the way and starting with a quill, you will have to cut it. A turkey or goose quill is what you want—use a sharp knife or blade and cut the quill as I have shown you on this page.

Mitchell Steel Nib

PEN LETTERING

See what I mean about hair lines and broad strokes? Try it—get used to the feeling of the pen and what the nib can do.

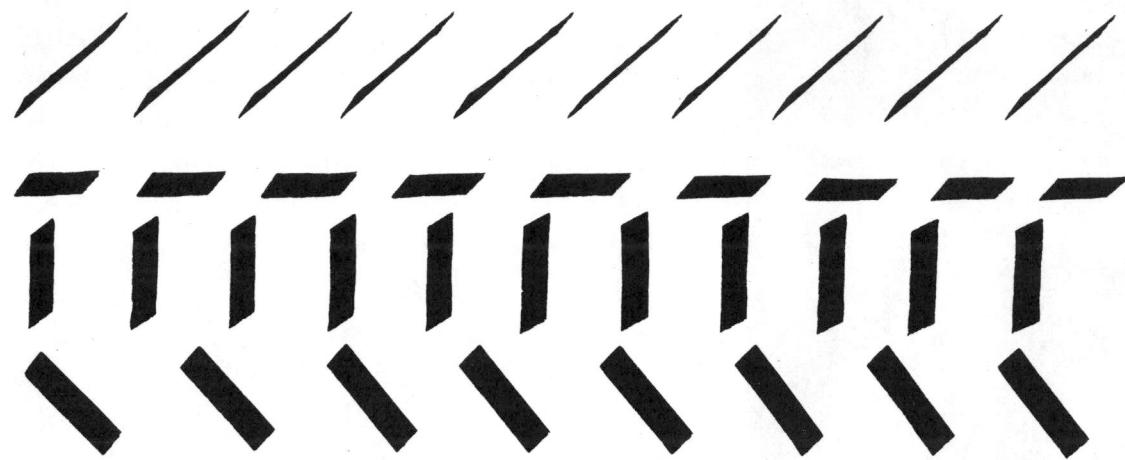

When you feel you can draw a straight line well, try a curve. You will soon find that the pen *has* to be used in this way. See if you can keep a number of curves the same size and shape. The pen nib moves, but the angle at which you hold it does not change.

Next, combine the straight strokes with the curves. The whole alphabet is open to you now. Try to keep the angle at which you hold the pen the same at all times.

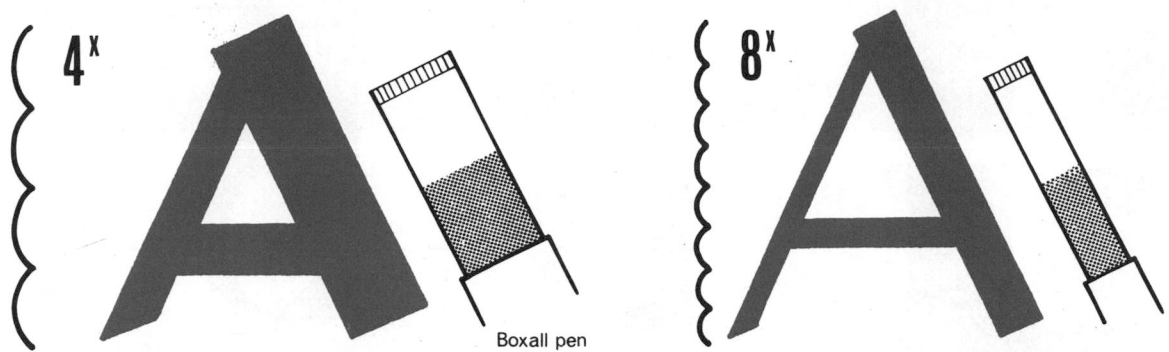

Boxall pen

Before you carry on, let's think briefly about the width of the pen. This, of course, will determine the width of the letter, because you will use only single strokes to build up the letter. Thus, A will be made up of three straights and B will be two straights and two curves. At the top of the page are two A's, both drawn in the same way and the same style, but the nib used for the letter on the left was twice as thick as that for the letter on the right. In other words, where on the left the letter height is 4 times the full width of the stroke, on the right the letter height is 8 times the width of the stroke. This gives two different 'weights' of letter. In the following alphabet I have used a nib like the one illustrated above and made the height of the letter 5 times the stoke width. You can tell by the width of the strokes what actions the pen must make and the order in which they should be made.

ABCDEFG

HIJKLMN

OPQRSTU

VWXYZ

Boxall pen

13

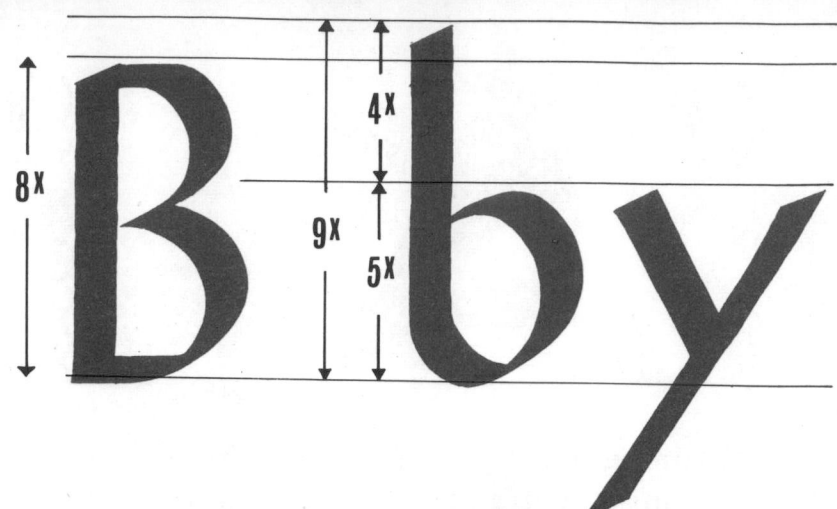

The *minuscule*, or small, letter is often referred to as *lower-case*. This is because the printer keeps his type in two cases, one higher than the other. The *upper case* has all the *capital letters* in it, and the small letters are all kept in the lower case.

These small letters are all derived from the capital letters, most of them being an abbreviated version of the same thing. They were developed to speed up writing. They are irregular letters as compared with the capitals; letters like b and d have rising strokes called *ascenders* and the letters like p and y have *descenders*. We aim to make the length of these ascenders and descenders nearly the same again as the letter height. The illustrations will show you exactly how. There is no rule about letter width, but a good principle is to make this sort of letter 5 pen widths high, with the ascenders going on to a height of 9 pen widths. Usually the descenders can be made a little longer.

a b c d e f g h i j
k l m n o p q r
s t u v w x y z

Boxall pen

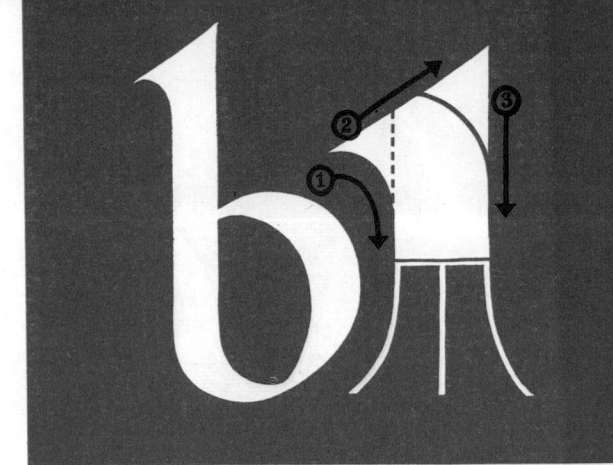

The Serif

The *serif* is the fine cross line found at the top and bottom of letters. Mostly used as decoration, it can, too, be of practical use. To read a whole book set in *sans-serif* type would be a strain; the serif gives a completeness to the letter which is generally found to be more satisfactory. Obviously there are many occasions when the sans-serif letter is preferable; we shall go into that later.

To use the serif in pen lettering is difficult, but worth trying—it would be wrong to talk about 'adding the serif', because we try to pen the letter so as to include the serif in the stroke. The illustration heading this page will show you just how to achieve this. The nib needs to be clean and free-flowing, as the serif must never appear heavy.

abcdefghij
klmnopqr
stuvwxyz

Graphos T nib

15

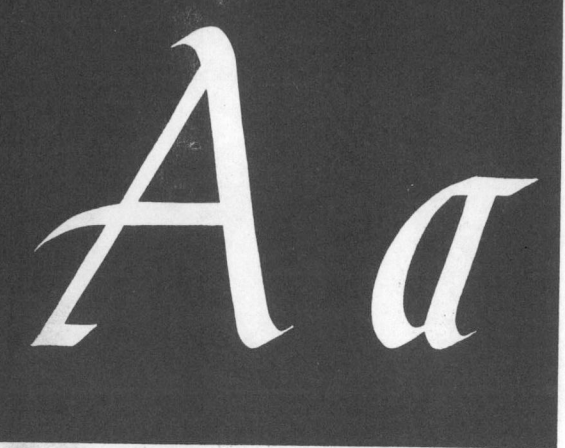

The Italic

This style of letter is a modification of the ordinary lower-case, minuscule, letter. Speed, and the need to get a lot of words into a space, led to a compression of the letter so that it was really based on an oval. The fifteenth-century Italian scribes, who constantly used this style of writing, are probably responsible for putting the slope to it. The lower-case letters in *italic* are sometimes quite different from the ordinary lower-case letters. Take g and a for example, and also compare the o and the d. The *italic capital*, on the other hand, is merely a sloping capital letter.

The danger with this style is to put too much of a slope on the letters. It's a good idea to check on this, to prevent the letters from progressively falling forward. On the opposite page I have written out both upper- and lower-case alphabets in the italic hand, using Mitchell nibs.

a a b b g g

Graphos T nib

abcdefghijklmn
opqrstuvwxyz

The Italic Alphabet

ABCDEFGHIJ
KLMNOPQ
RSTUVWXYZ

Mitchell steel nibs

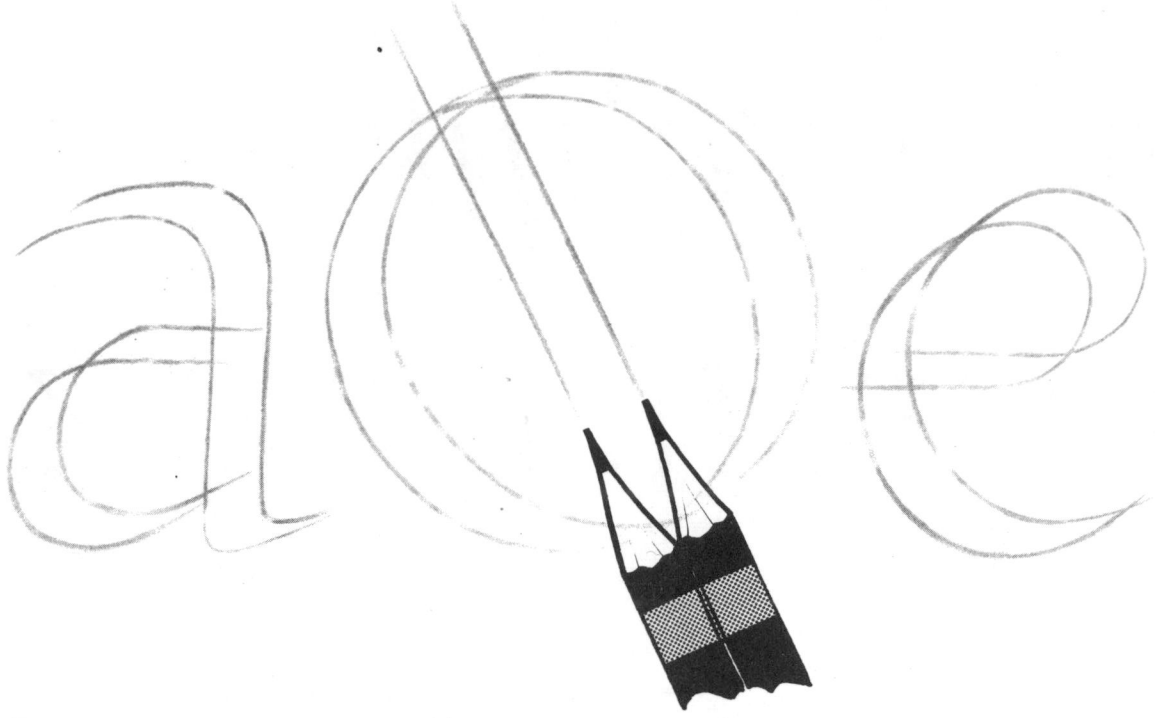

Pencils and Felt Tips

The process shown on this page always reminds me of the schoolboy trying to halve his work at writing out lines! It is probably not unknown to you. You tie two pencils together and what one writes—the other does, too. Here, I've used the idea to construct letters. The outcome is just like the effect with the broad-nibbed pen, but the letters are even bigger. If it does nothing else, this method will give you excellent practice in controlling your writing. The example above was done just as I have drawn it, using two soft pencils held together with sticky tape.

On the market for some time now has been a pen with a thick felt tip —these felt tips come in various widths and styles and are soaked with a special fluid that smells horrible, but gives really excellent results. I have been using these Flo-Master pens for various purposes for years. The resultant lettering can be seen here.

Having got so far, it is as well that you should know the technical terms for the parts of the letter. The opposite page should tell you all you want to know.

Flo-Master felt tip

Parts of the Letter

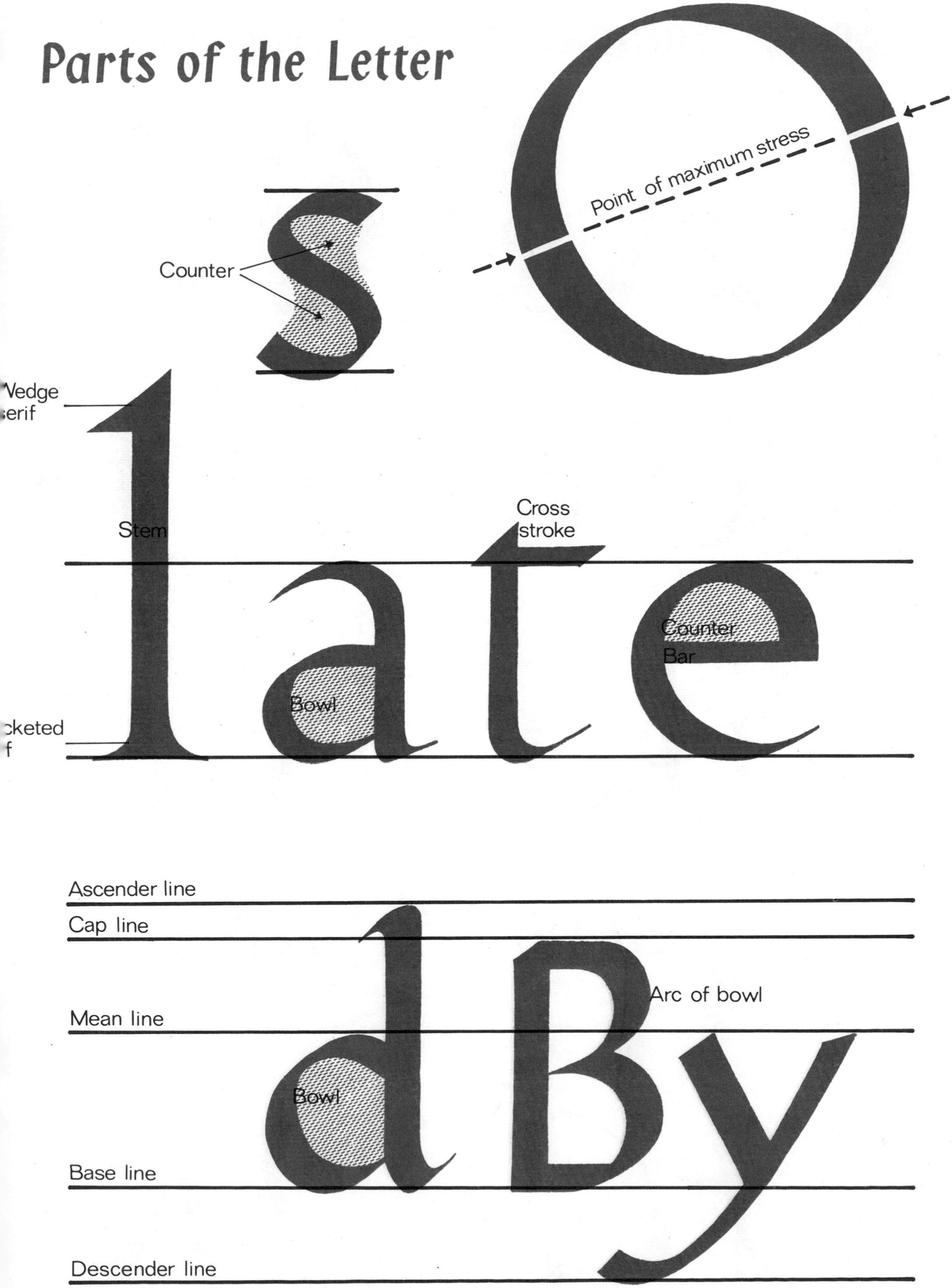

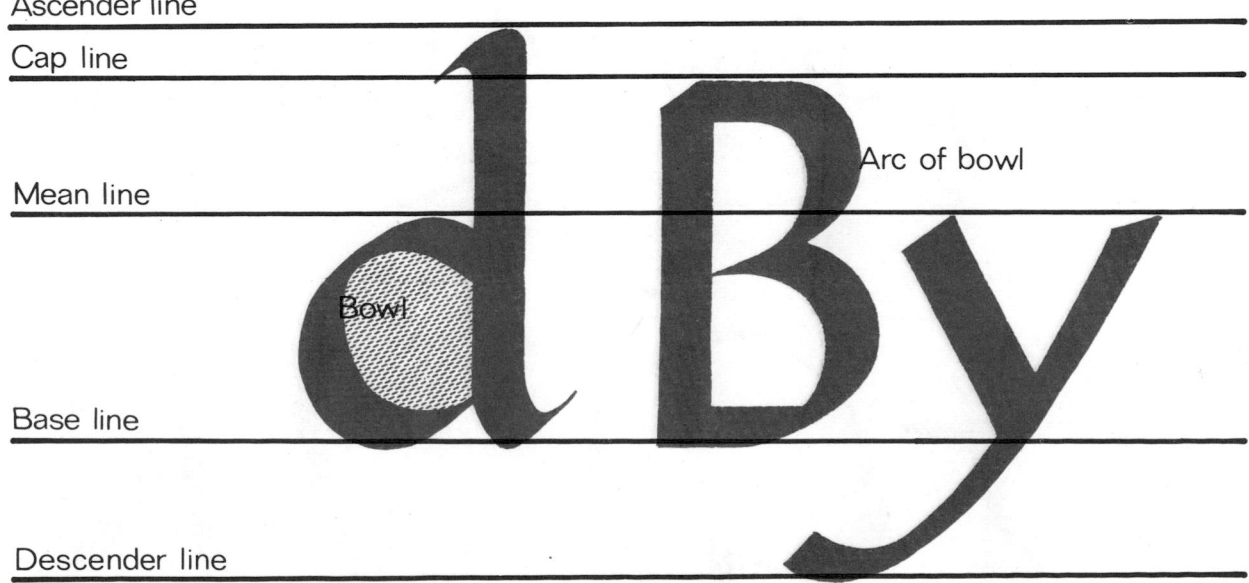

Counter

Point of maximum stress

Wedge serif

Stem

Cross stroke

Counter

Bar

Bowl

Bracketed serif

Ascender line

Cap line

Arc of bowl

Mean line

Bowl

Base line

Descender line

Gothic

Graphos T nib

It is reasonable to suggest that there are five *styles* of lettering—Roman and Italic, which we have been working at, and Block, Script and Gothic. All the others are variations. As a means of pen lettering, *Gothic* is fascinating. It has a heavy dignity that makes it very pleasant to use. On the other hand, there are limited uses for this style of lettering. It is Germanic in origin and often used in its many forms in hymn books, on church notice-boards, for the text of certificates and wherever an aura of dignity seems indicated.

These examples show some Gothic letters made of straight strokes only and some where a mixture of straights, curves and curlicues makes a fascinating, if complicated, letter.

Script means writing. It can be type imitating hand writing, or the form of writing that is done with a very fine pen. You can still see it used on some visiting cards and invitations. There is a printed example on page 59. Writing like this, called 'copy-book script', used to be taught, but is now considered old-fashioned and a rather better form of pen lettering with a spade nib is preferred.

Graphos T nib

abcdefghijklm
opqrstuvwxyz

Extreme care must be taken when using the Gothic letter to see that it is legible—sometimes the similarity and profusion of down strokes make for rather difficult reading. Look at the lower-case letters m, n, u, v, for example—and take a word like minute !

The effect of Gothic capitals, which are splendid as initial letters for illuminated manuscripts, can go completely haywire if they are used together. Take the example of the photo above, showing writing on a board outside a church. Can you read it easily?

ILLEGIBLE
illegible

VERSAL

Mitchell steel nib

This is a rather lovely capital letter, but like the Gothic letter must be used sparingly. Chapter headings and initials are cases where you might use it. I used it myself recently on the opening titles for a TV play about Joan of Arc. The use of it, very sparingly, on the television screen was quite effective.

To pen this letter, you need a finer nib than those we have used before, but still a spade nib. The work is increased on *Versal* letters, because the down strokes are formed from two strokes, and you make them thin in the middle and wider at the top and bottom. Whether you fill in the letters or leave them open is up to you—do whatever seems best in the circumstances.

One thing I will say and it is this: in Versal we are approaching the art of drawn lettering, although still using a pen, and it is necessary to have some knowledge of the construction of the roman letter in order to do this job properly. It would be well to have a good look at the letter proportions on pages 26 and 34 and also to get an idea of the characteristics of the roman letter from pages 36-41.

Have a try at some Versal anyway, and before it breaks your heart, turn to the following page and have a bit of fun.

ABCDEFGHI
JKLMNOPQ
RSTUVWXYZ

Decoration

I don't think, somehow, that you are going to use this form of penmanship very much! However, like all other unusual letter forms, it has a place from time to time. The beautifully written manuscripts of earlier *calligraphers* would have lost something without the embellishments that this form of decoration can give.

Just as the Roman inscription on the Trajan Column in Rome is asserted to be the finest example of classic roman lettering, so the writing in the *Book of Kells* has the same reputation as an example of pen lettering. This ancient book contains, along with local records, copies of the Gospels in Latin, and dates from the eighth century. The original is kept in the library of Trinity College, Dublin, in Ireland.

Detail from the 'Book of Kells'

By permission of the Board of Trinity College, Dublin

Simple Capitals

Like most things that look clean, tidy and simple, the '*simple*' *capital alphabet* is really quite difficult to pen. First, it is of a uniform or *cord line*. There are no thick and thin strokes. To achieve this, something like a Graphos rounded nib is required. You can see just what this looks like on the page, and what it does. The Graphos has the advantage of being a fountain pen with interchangeable nibs, so no constant refilling is required. Held at an angle of 40 degrees the pen, when pressed lightly on the paper, produces a small circle. Thus any stroke—made at any angle—will have a uniform thickness.

As you have already had a look at the proportions of these capitals on the next page, you should start experimenting with the rounded pen and achieve some straight and some curved strokes.

ABCDEFG
HIJKLMN
OPQRSTU
VWXYZ

Graphos O nib

$1\frac{1}{1}$	OQCGD
$3\frac{3}{4}$	AHTNU
$3\frac{3}{4}$	XYZ
$1\frac{1}{2}$	SEFBLP
Miscellaneous	KIJRWM

LETTER SIZES AND PROPORTION

In the roman alphabet, we can categorize the letters according to *width* sizes. The simplest way to think of these sizes is as divisions of a square, wide letters occupying a whole square, mediums taking three-quarters of the square and narrow ones, half of the square. There are some six letters in the alphabet which could perhaps be classed under these headings also, but which I prefer to put under a separate heading of 'miscellaneous sizes', and in the pages following the chapter on drawn lettering I will fully explain why.

As all letters must appear to be of the same *height*, a little cheating has to be done! It is a fact that if you draw an E and an O, side by side, of exactly the same height, the E will appear taller. This is an optical illusion, brought about because the O only *just* touches the capital and base lines. This is true of the A as well, but only where it touches the capital line. Another illusion concerns the central position of the bar in F, E and H. It is usually drawn just above the centre.

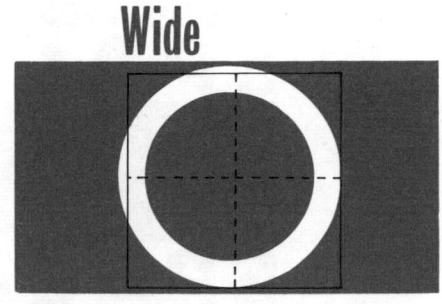

Wide

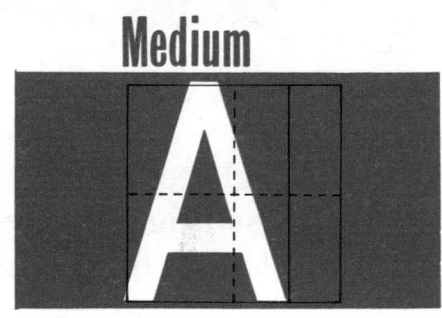

Medium

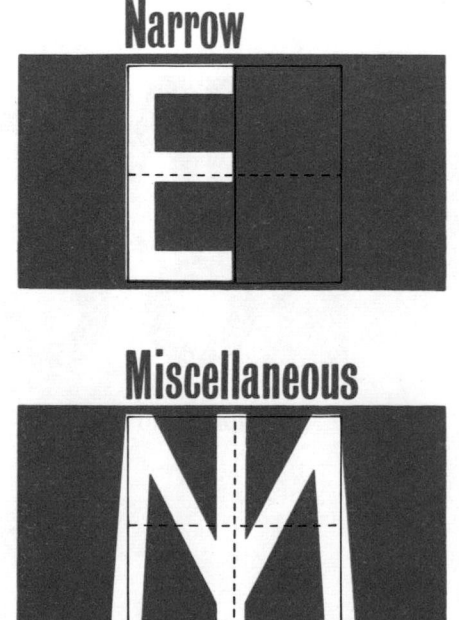

Narrow

Miscellaneous

Spacing

SPACING OF CAPITALS

SPACING OF CAPITALS

It is very important how you space the individual letters that go to make up a word. There's no rule—different letters will have different spaces between them. You must work by eye; if it doesn't look right, then it isn't right. Correct spacing is as important as the correct drawing of the letters, for it is part of the design of the full word.

The two best examples of this occur when two curves come together —for instance, two O's—and when two vertical lines come together as in the case of I's and H's. At the bottom of the page, you will see how this applies to the two words, HIM and ROOM. We try to achieve a correct balance with an *apparently* equal amount of space between the letters.

The words SPACING OF CAPITALS, if they have equal spacing between the letters, tend to look wrong. You can see how to correct this inequality.

Futura Bold

TELEVISION TELEVISION

THIS IS TELEVISION
THIS IS TELEVISION

The importance of spacing applies as much to word spacing as it does to letter spacing. Again, it is a matter of balance. The area in which you have to work determines the size of letters. Here, too, it all comes back to spacing. The word TELEVISION at the top left of the page is properly lettered, properly letter-spaced, but badly placed. The example on the right is better. It is the same thing but smaller, and allows us to see the word properly and in a more attractive setting. The spacing of words shown on this page speaks for itself.

When words are placed one below the other, as they might be in a poster, it is usual to position them symmetrically. You should always rule a vertical line down the centre of the paper, as this will help you in placing the letters.

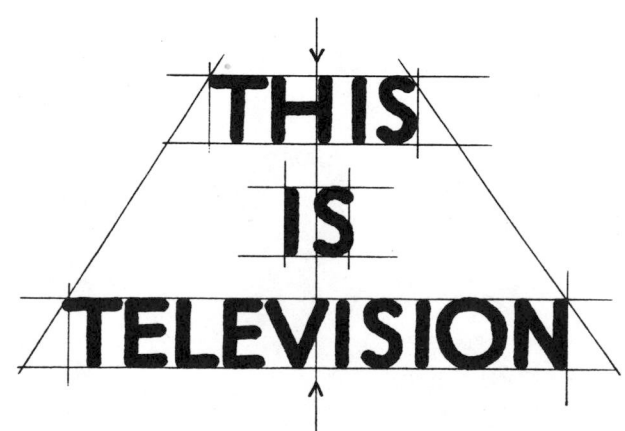

Graphos O nibs 29

PEN NUMERALS

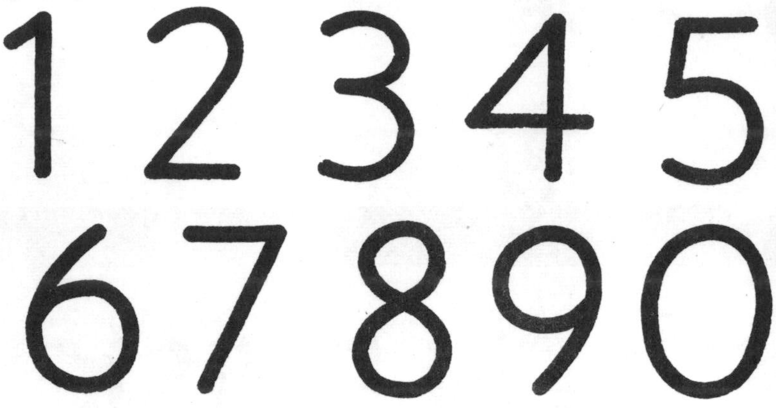

1 2 3 4 5
6 7 8 9 0

Graphos O nib

We use Arabic numerals, and sets have been designed to fit in with our different forms of lettering. Here, I have shown you one set of numerals that can be used with the letters shown on page 25. These are drawn with the Graphos round-point pen. The other set of numerals you would use in combination with lettering such as that shown on pages 13 and 14. Here the nib is one of the 'spade' type.

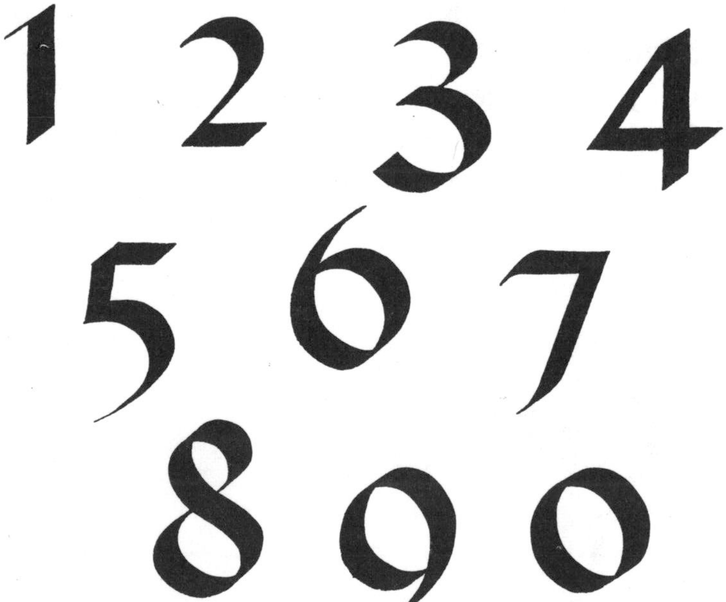

1 2 3 4
5 6 7
8 9 0

Spade nib-Graphos T

30

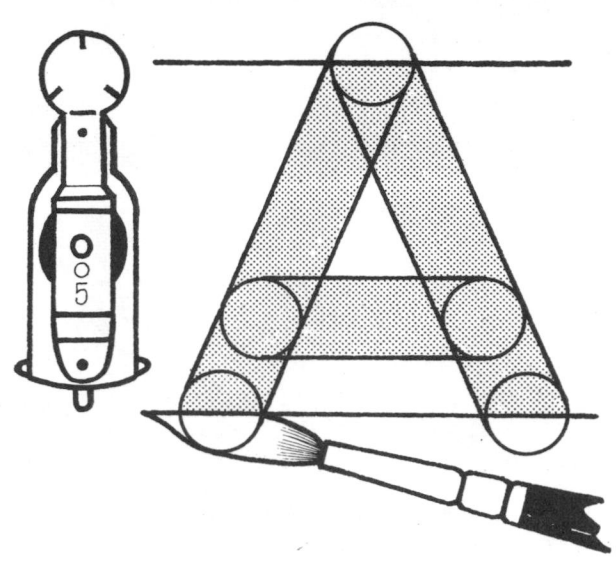

BLOCK LETTERS

This is really our simple capital alphabet, tidied up a bit. As you see, the rounded end to the letter, which characterized the round-nib letter, has disappeared and the end is now square and clean-cut. This marks the turning-point between the calligrapher's pen letter and the drawn letter. The pen letter is adapted by using a brush and white paint to 'cut off' the rounded end. Of course, this same letter can be drawn up, in pencil, then painted or inked in with a brush.

With the knowledge you now have of letter sizes and spacing, you will be able to make a splendid alphabet in this style.

ABCDEFGHIJ
KLMNOPQR
STUVWXYZ

Graphos O and brush

31

DRAWN LETTERING

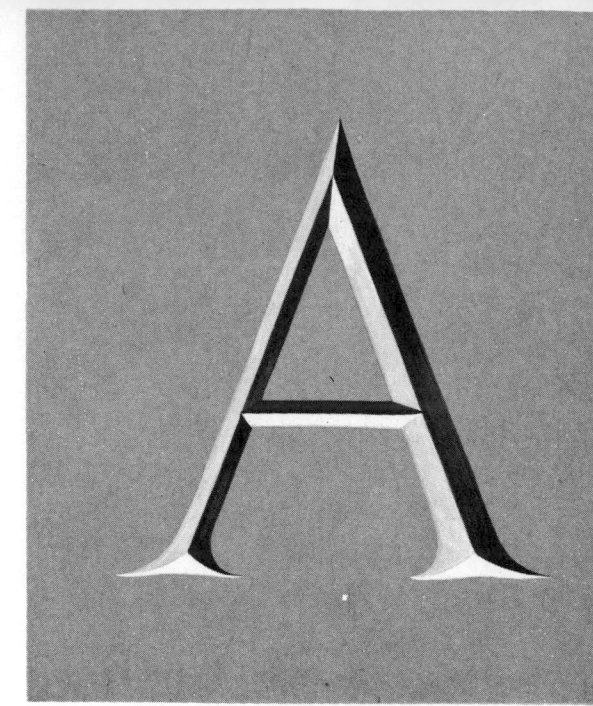

Just as the examples of pen lettering you see have a character all their own, so too have letters that have been drawn with a brush. The lettering that is going to occupy the following pages is called *Trajan Roman*. Although we are used to seeing examples of it printed on paper or painted over shops, etc., it was originally carved out of stone. The photograph on page 2, the frontispiece, shows you a part of this beautiful lettering which was inscribed about A.D. 113 and commemorated the erection of a monument to the Roman Emperor, Trajan. Because of the immense size of this job, the stone-cutter made slight differences in the sizes of some of the letters. This he did purposely, so that people looking up at the inscription would see it to its best advantage. The Victoria and Albert Museum, in London, has a brilliant cast copy of this inscription. It has been pointed out, however, that photographs of it show minute distortions. It's as well to know this, but it certainly will not make any difference to your enjoyment of what has very rightly been called the finest achievement in lettering.

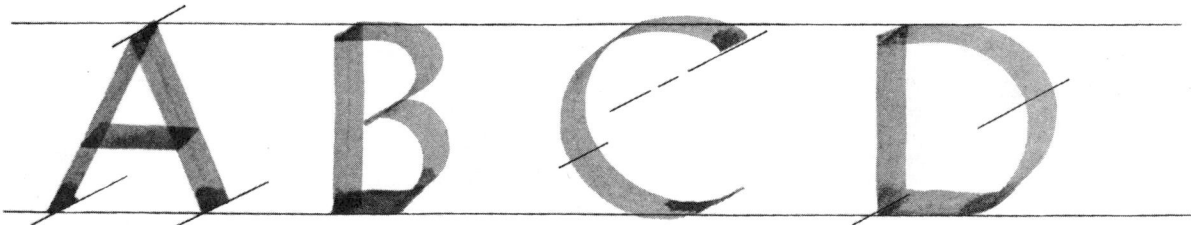

Boxall pen and diluted ink

As it was originally cut in stone, it will be well to see how the craft of the stone-cutter has given the roman letter its characteristic form and how, retaining that, we can now draw this letter and achieve a similar effect with the brush.

The three A's on this page show how a progression has come about from the original incised letter that copied the pen letter, to the serif letter we know as Trajan Roman. Letter (a) is cut just as if a spade nib had penned it. In (b), the letter has had horizontal cuts made to the letter ends, so that the letter stands firmly on a line. In (c) the triangular cut has been extended at the base line and has formed a serif. This had a practical purpose. It was difficult to make that square end, it often got chipped away and cleaning it up resulted in a serif. This looked pretty good, so it was exaggerated and became as we see it now.

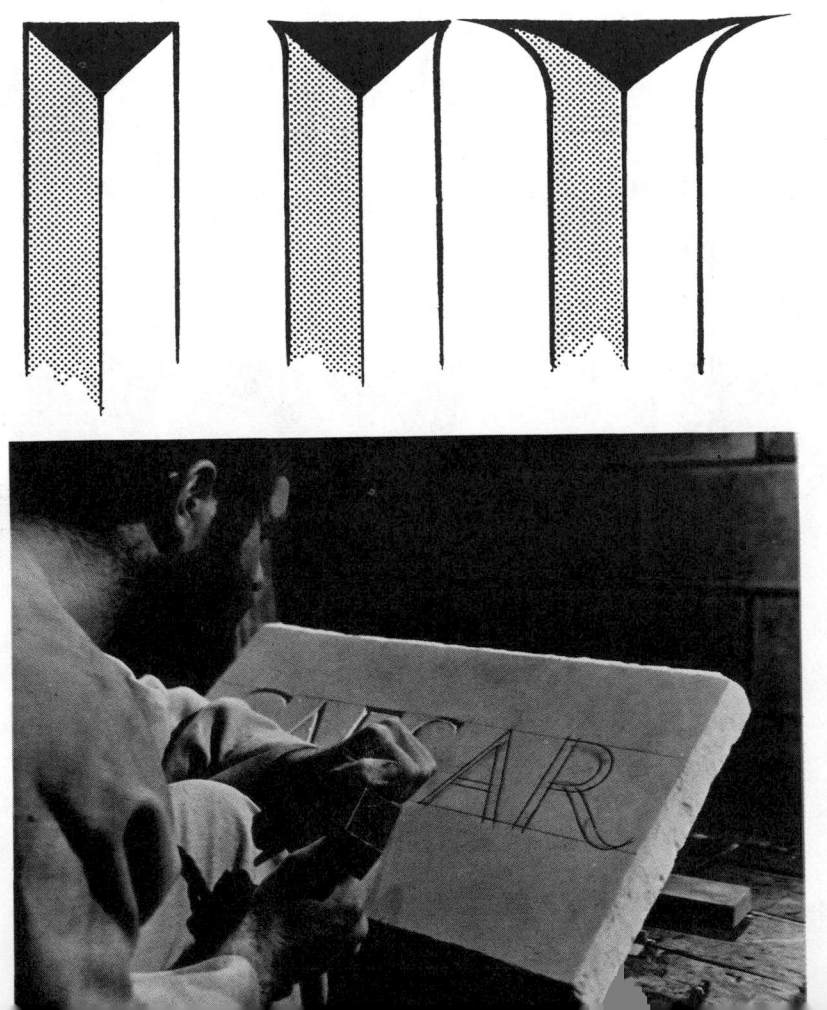

a

b

c   Brush and ruling pen

ABCDE
FGILM
NOPQ
RSTVX

Sable brush no.4

Roman Capitals

Here then is the Trajan Roman alphabet, drawn with the brush and emulating the incised letter. I have used a pointed brush here, filling in the letter, having previously drawn it with a soft pencil. The pencilled letter is a guide only; it will give the proportion of the letter and widths of thicks and thins. They will be drawn free hand—no rulers or compasses used, except to rule the base, centre and capital lines. The brush, of course, is used free hand with the minimum of brush strokes. One of the delights of the drawn letter is that it *looks drawn*. It should never look mechanical, as it would if a ruler had been employed. To give an equality to letter forms, the thickest parts of curved letters are made slightly wider than the vertical strokes—and the straight strokes are made slightly concave at the waist or middle. Look back to pages 26 and 27 to check on proportions and letter sizes.

The letters shown on this page were not originally included in the alphabet as used on the Trajan Column, but have been designed to conform to the original letters, some being borrowed from Greek and Semitic sources. In the Romans' alphabet, for example, the name JULIUS was written IVLIVS.

Sable brush no.4

A ¾ or medium letter. The cross stroke is half the width of the wide stroke. Variations of the apex, or tip, can be used if and when they seem appropriate. If the Trajan apex is used, the point should extend above the capital line.

A ½ or narrow letter. Be careful to make this letter neither too narrow nor too wide. The latter will make the bowls appear fat! The stroke attaching the two bowls is placed just over the centre line. Note the angle at the top of the upper bowl and the curve at the base.

A ¹⁄₁ or wide letter. The curves project above and below the base and capital lines; C is not a 'cut-off'. The top and bottom arms are slightly flattened. The thickest part of the curve is below the centre line.

A ¹⁄₁ or wide letter. As with C, the top and bottom flatten out slightly to join the upright. It is angled at the top, curved at the base. The thickest part of the curve is above the centre line.

Sable brush no. 6

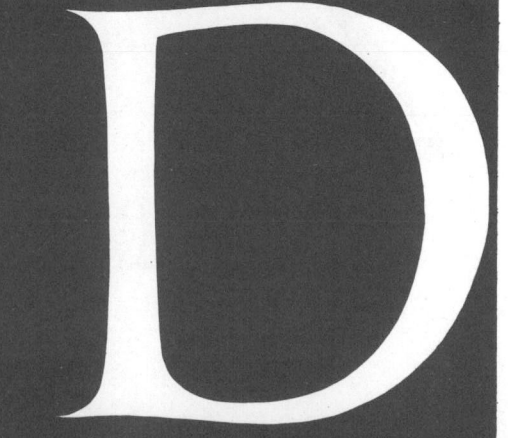

A ½ or narrow letter. Never make E too wide. It is really twice as high as it is wide. The bar is drawn just above the centre line. The serifs can be prolonged, but be careful not to give it a 'closed-in' feeling. The bottom arm may be extended in a flourish, possibly when preceding T.

A ½ or narrow letter: the same as E but with the bottom arm missing. The bar is drawn just over, or sometimes at the centre line. Do not make it too short.

A ½ or wide letter. As with C, the top arm flattens slightly. The bottom arm angles to the stem. The stem rises almost to the centre line. The stem may descend below the base line and end with a tail flourish.

A ¾ or medium letter. It can err on the wide side, but be careful! The cross bar should be placed above centre and made slightly thinner in the middle. H does not appear in Trajan Roman, but was used in other Roman inscriptions.

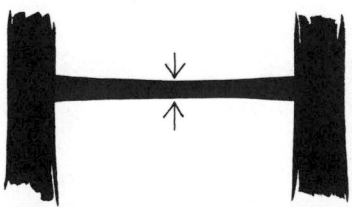

A miscellaneous letter in width, as is J, although probably the most important letter, being the basis of all the uprights. J was not used by the Romans—the two forms shown can be drawn, the extended I form being, perhaps, more attractive.

Another miscellaneous letter—more wide than medium. It was not used in Trajan Roman. This letter can be most attractive, with the extended diagonal stroke ending in a flourish. Three versions are shown. Note the different placings of the wide diagonal stroke.

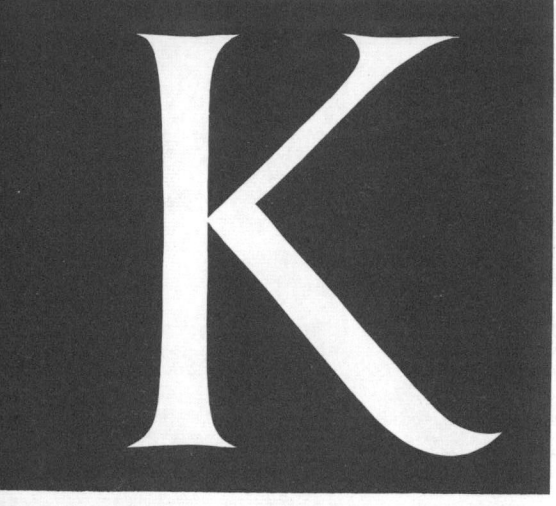

A ½ or narrow letter. Preceding A, the thin stroke should be shortened slightly. Preceding T, it should be extended.

A 1/1 or wide letter. In fact, it can be more a 'miscellaneous' letter, erring on the wide side, as the legs can be splayed out. The Trajan M has no serifs at the capital line, but these may be drawn. The legs may also be drawn vertically. The V of the letter projects below the base line only in the Trajan letter. The upright strokes would project in this way if no serifs were drawn.

A ¾ or medium letter. If you draw N in the Trajan manner, it will have only two serifs. It is often drawn with three. It can also be drawn with a flourish at the left. Be careful not to make the uprights too thin.

A ¼ or wide letter. It is theoretically a circle, although in the Trajan it appears slightly compressed. Watch the position of the thickest points. Q is another O, but with a carefully drawn tail. The following letter will determine the style of the tail. Note it in the Trajan inscription.

A ½ or narrow letter—very difficult this. Both its forms have their attraction but the open bowl, where the curve does not join the stem, is particularly pleasant if given the correct point.

A miscellaneous letter in size. This is not P with a tail, but more like B with a larger bowl. The tail emerges from the curved bowl at a near right angle and finishes in a variety of ways. The large Trajan example obviously gave subsequent designers the model for the K we now use.

A ½ or narrow letter. It is built up of two circles, the top one slightly smaller than the lower one. Do not, however, draw two circles and link them. The action must swing from the top to the lower arm, describing the two curves with the maximum stress at the centre. Following V or preceding A, the S can be sloped slightly forward.

A ¾ or medium letter. T is an I with a cross stroke. This stroke must be varied to suit the occasion. The Trajan has a subtle serif, as you see. If T were followed by W, it would be in order to extend the cross stroke at the left.

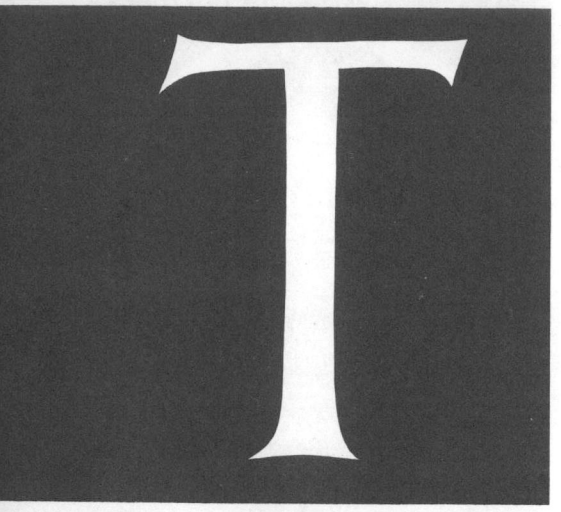

A ¾ or medium letter. It was not used in Trajan Roman (see V). Three satisfactory styles have been used and it is up to you to employ the one best suited to your needs.

A ¾ or medium letter. The Roman V stood for both V and U; later it was used in a pair to represent W. The thicker stem is sometimes curved in a flourish, without the serif.

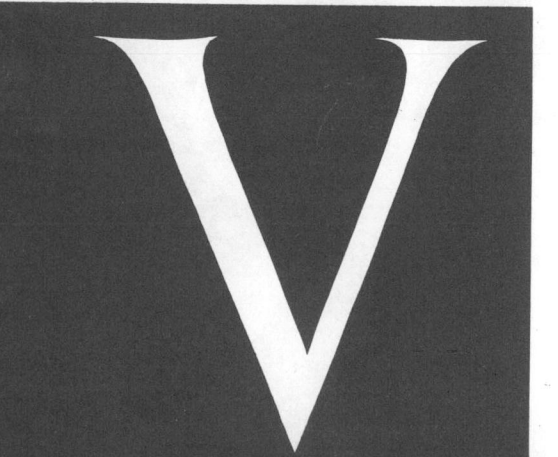

A miscellaneous letter. Like M, W is over-wide. Originally made of two V's, it was actually printed as VV. Several forms have been designed, the larger one shown here being, perhaps, the most used. It also looks well when the pointed apex at the centre goes slightly over the capital line.

A $\frac{3}{4}$ or medium letter, a very difficult letter to draw. The cross-piece is slightly over centre, so as to give the effect of both counters being equal.

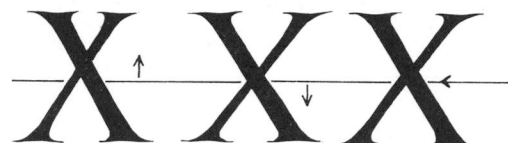

A $\frac{3}{4}$ or medium letter, not used in Trajan Roman. The point of the counter does not quite reach the centre line. Do not spread the arms too much. Be wary of using unorthodox designs, although the one shown here can be pleasing.

A $\frac{3}{4}$ or medium letter. Like Y, Z has been borrowed from the Greek alphabet and is not used in Trajan Roman. Z is an interesting letter, because the diagonal line breaks the 'thick-thin' rule. Actually it should be thin, but this would look absurd, as you can see.

Minuscule Letters

We have already seen how the minuscule or lower-case letters evolved between the second and the ninth centuries. We are quite at home with these letters, as we see them every day in books, papers and magazines. The alphabet shown on the opposite page is the one which harmonizes best with the Trajan Roman of the preceding pages. It has developed from the pen writing of the scribes and can be readily compared with the lower-case alphabets shown on pages 14 and 15. In this case, the letters are brush-drawn and follow the style used in Trajan Roman.

It is on this style of lettering that most of our modern type faces have been based. The words *type face* describe the letter as it is used in printing, the lead, back-to-front, letter that is inked and pressed on paper so as to leave its mark.

The use of printing brought about new designs in letters. This was because the type-cutters found it convenient to make particular cuts with their type-cutting tools. For instance, it seems reasonable that with a gouging tool, some strokes should be finished off with a circle. So we get circular dots over i and often we find this circle applied to letters like **a f r**. Stone-cutters, too, can achieve this circular cut—so it is reasonable to apply it to *our* minuscule alphabet here.

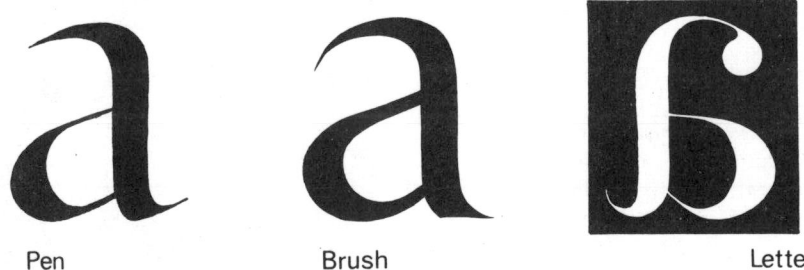

Pen   Brush   Letter cutting tool

abcdefg
hijklmn
opqrstu
vwxyz

Sable brush no.6

Numerals

The Romans, as we know, had a system of numerals which was based on their alphabet symbols, I, V, X, representing 1, 5, 10—we see this every day on many clocks. Big Ben, the world's most famous clock, has Roman numerals. The main reason for using these on clock faces is that they make a better design when placed about a circle than do Arabic figures. The Romans used L, C, D and M to denote 50, 100, 500 and 1000. One of the few occasions these are used today is in showing the date of a film. You can see this on the cinema screen among the credit titles for a film, with 1965 appearing as MCMLXV.

As in the case of the minuscule letters on the preceding page, the numerals below have been designed to harmonize with the Trajan Roman.

The symbols we use today to represent the numbers 1 to 10 are Arabic, or have evolved from the Arabic. You can recognize this most easily in looking at ١٢٣. Turn the page sideways and you will see what is meant.

1 2 3 4 5
6 7 8 9 0

1 2 3 4 5 6 7 8 9 0

Sometimes where numerals are drawn or incised in conjunction with the Trajan Roman alphabet, the piece of work has been made more beautiful by the figures being made of unequal height. This style of numeral is known as *old-style* and is shown above. You can often see it used on commemoration tablets and memorial stones. This *non-lining* figure is seldom, if ever, used in printing. The type face of all numerals is of equal height and known as *modern*.

Other symbols that have now become familiar to us are adapted similarly. On this page you can see some variations, all used with Trajan Roman. From what you now know of this alphabet, you will begin to understand which of the different designs to use with it in a given circumstance.

Practical Lettering

Now when you try your hand at some practical drawn lettering, you should make the result as pleasing as possible. This means that, apart from the letters themselves, the placing and spacing must be right. To help you achieve this, the job in hand should be drawn out roughly on tracing paper. You can then arrange the spacing satisfactorily. Check the width of letters and tidy up generally before starting the finished job.

The pictures on this page are to help you achieve a correct layout without having to alter the finished work. At (a), the letters have been positioned on tracing paper. Guide lines are there to help. Make any corrections and proceed to (b): the trace is turned over and the lettering, seen in reverse, is pencilled or chalked over. When the finished work is being painted with a light colour on a dark background, use white chalk or conté pencil. For dark lettering on a light background, black chalk or soft lead pencil should be used. Next, (c) shows how the trace is laid down on the working surface. It can be moved about until you have it properly positioned. In this case it should be in the centre. Now, with a hard pencil, the lettering is traced on to the working surface. Lastly, at (d), the lettering is filled in and finished with a brush.

46

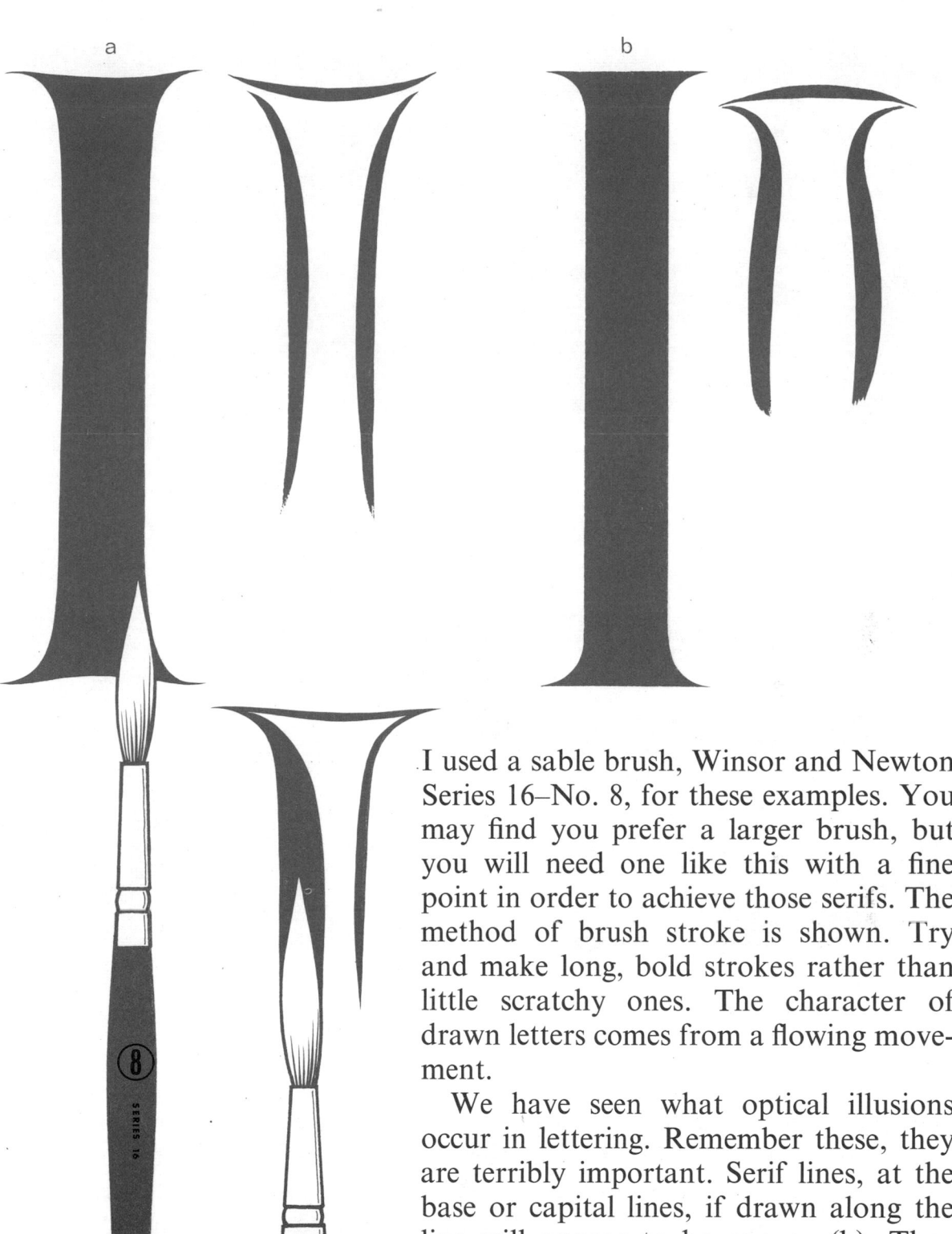

a

b

I used a sable brush, Winsor and Newton Series 16–No. 8, for these examples. You may find you prefer a larger brush, but you will need one like this with a fine point in order to achieve those serifs. The method of brush stroke is shown. Try and make long, bold strokes rather than little scratchy ones. The character of drawn letters comes from a flowing movement.

We have seen what optical illusions occur in lettering. Remember these, they are terribly important. Serif lines, at the base or capital lines, if drawn along the line will appear to be convex (b). They must have a subtle curve in order to look right, as at (a). Again, should the stem lines be drawn parallel (b), they will appear to bulge. They must be tapered at the waist—see (a).

Sable brush no. 4 - black and white poster paint

The paper or board on which you are going to draw the lettering will do a great deal to help or hinder the appearance of your work. For instance, black lettering on white will never cause any complaints, but black on dark grey wouldn't show up too well. Colours, too, must be carefully chosen; and until you have some experience of this craft, I should stick to lettering in black or white, while experimenting with varying types and textures of background. The film and television industry uses some interesting backgrounds on which to display lettered titles—look out for them.

48

LETTER GROUPS AND TYPES

I suppose there must be more of 'the printed word' than of anything else ever invented by man. So it is not surprising that the letters involved undergo changes of design from time to time. At the moment, we have discovered that from the point of view of legibility and good design, there are four main groups of letters. They comprise *old face*, *modern face*, *sans serif* and *slab serif*. The 'old face', as a type face, is nearest to the letters we've been dealing with, developed by typographers from the calligraphers' pen letters and the Roman inscriptions.

The 'modern' has a fuller down stroke and the serifs have become hair lines.

The 'sans-serif'—'without serif'—type goes back to the earliest roman letter, but has become better proportioned. This sort of face is often used for easy legibility and where fewer words are required than in, say, a newspaper.

'Slab serif', with its solid, thick serifs, seems well designed for modern use in posters, playbills and shop fronts and by commercial organizations.

On the following pages you can see a number of varieties of each of these type faces and some of the uses for which they are best suited.

| Old face | Modern | Sans Serif | Slab Serif |

PERPETUA TITLING

This type face designed by Eric Gill appears as a Capital Letter only. 'Titling', as the name implies, is used when comparatively few words are to be used for some important purpose.

Compare this type with the Trajan alphabet. The designer has thickened the down strokes and made each letter suitable for the mechanical method of reproduction. It is easily distinguished as being derived from the Classical Roman. This is grouped as 'Old Face'.

You will find this type face used successfully whenever a feeling of dignity is required. Look for it on the facade of Banks, etc.

ABCDEFGHIJ
JKLMNOPQ
RRSTUUUV
WXYZ&£123
4567890.,!?"'()

'Monotype' Series 258

Bembo

Another 'Old Face'. Perhaps the finest example of Upper and Lower Case Type; certainly it is, historically speaking, the oldest.
Note the bracketed serifs and compare with the penned serifs on page 15. *The Italic, Upper and Lower Case, is quite beautiful and achieves a hand drawn quality with the advantages of being a mechanical type.*
An excellent face for large areas of type in the smaller points as seen in books.

ABCDEFGHIJKLMNO
PQRSTUVWXYZ&
abcdefghijklmnopqrstuv
wxyz*ABCDEFGHIJKL*
MNOPQRSTUVWXY
Z&abcdefghijklmnopqrstuv
wxyz1234567890.,!?([£
1234567890.,!?

'Monotype' Series 270

Garamond

This is Garamond Bold. Bold means that the type is heavier, or thicker, than usual. Compare this with Bembo.
This is a good face to use when the printing process does not allow for a really hard black; as in photolitho printing.
Again, this is an 'Old Face' derived from the Classical Roman forms. It looks well used as a Display letter.

ABCDEFGHIJKLMN
OPQRSTUVWXYZab
cdefghijklmnopqrstuvw
xyz&£1234567890
ABCDEFGHIJKLMN
OPQRSTUVWXYZab
cdefghijklmnopqrstuvx
yz&£1234567890

Walbaum

Like Bodoni, Walbaum is a Modern Face and has basic similarities. It gives an impression of squareness in the letters and is more open in appearance than Bodoni. It is very good used for large areas of small type.

ABCDEFGHIJKLMNOPQR
STUVWXYZabcdefghijklm
nopqrstuvwxyz*ABCDEF*
GHIJKLMNOPQRSTUV
WXYZabcdefghijklmnop
qrstuvwxyz&£1234567890
£1234567890

Bodoni

This is called a 'Modern Face'. The obvious characteristic is the point of Maximum Stress which is vertical; straight up and down. There is a great contrast between thick and thin strokes. The serifs are hairlines and usually unbracketed.
This face is Bodoni Bold. There is a less heavy face – Bodoni. And one heavier called **Bodoni Ultra Bold.** Look for Bodoni Ultra Bold used in Display, Shopfronts, etc.
The least heavy Bodoni is suitable for larger areas of type.

ABCDEFGHIJKLMNO
PQRSTUVWXYZabcde
fghijklmnopqrstuvwxyz
&£1234567890*ABCDE*
FGHIJKLMNOPQRS
TUVWXYZ&£1234567
890

Rockwell

This Face is called 'Slab Serif', or Egyptian, because the serifs are about the same thickness as the stems, this is the obvious characteristic.
There are many weights of Rockwell and **there are two condensed alphabets.** The light weight can be used for books and magazines over large areas of type but for comfortable reading the Old and Modern Faces cannot be beaten. It is a good Display letter, especially in its **Bold Face.**

ABCDEFGHIJKLMN
OPQRSTUVWXYZab
cdefghijklmnopqrstu
vwxyz&£1234567890
ABCDEFGHIJKLMN
OPQRSTUVWXYZab
cdefghijklmnopqrst
uvwxyz&1234567890

grotesque

The 'Sans Serif' Letter is literally 'Without Serif' and there are many examples; the most well known being Eric Gill's 'Gill Sans'. This Face is Grotesque Condensed; it has been squeezed into a thinner letter. **Ordinary Grotesque can be used for fairly large areas of type in magazines, etc. It would be tiring to read a book printed in this face.**
Grotesque Condensed is excellent for Display purposes and for Television.

ABCDEFGHIJKLMNOPQRST
UVWXYZ&abcdefghijklmno
pqrstuvwxyz£1234567890
,,;;!?"-([—

univers

Another 'Sans Serif' is Univers—a good legible letter form in both Upper and Lower Case. It is especially suitable for learning to read. Univers comes in Light, Medium, **Bold** and **Extra Bold**. Its versatility makes it suitable for practically all purposes other than a complete book.

ABCDEFGHIJKLMNOP
QRSTUVWXYZabcdefg
hijklmnopqrstuvwxyz&
£1234567890.,!?''([

ABCDEFGHIJKLMNOP
QRSTUVWXYZabcdefg
hijklmnopqrstuvwxyz&
£1234567890.,!?''([

'Monotype' Series 693

HAND-PRINTED LETTERS

On the previous pages, you have seen some examples of the best in typography. The letter faces shown were designed to be reproduced mechanically. But there are occasions when a hand-printed letter is desirable; it may well fill the bill better than a drawn letter. The reason for this is that the very medium of printing brings about its own characteristics. The simplest way of printing a letter is to cut a potato in half and on the flat surface, cut away the bits you don't want to appear in print—my illustrations will make this method clear. Similar cuts can be made from lino, wood or rubber. This is a craft on its own, but I think this book would not be complete without a mention of the fascinating subject of hand printing. To make the print, you will first have to press the cut either on to a thin film of ink rolled out on glass, or on to an ink pad. Another way is to paint the cut itself by brush with poster paint before pressing it to paper.

There is a splendid book published by Wm. R. Scott, Inc., called *Paper Ink and Roller,* which tells you absolutely everything you could want to know about making prints.

Print to paper

Paper to print

Potato cut

58

RIGHT AND WRONG USE OF LETTERING

There is little point in being able to draw good lettering if you fail to appreciate what sorts of lettering should be used for specific purposes. Here is a commercial artist's drawing for a pamphlet. It advertises heavy industry. You, as a letterer, have the job of adding in 'Heavy Industry'. Would you use the type that I have? Of course you wouldn't. Having seen several types now, which would *you* choose?

HEAVY INDUSTRY

The drawing and the idea suggest a bold, heavy letter. There is no room for a wide letter, so you might perhaps choose Compacta. Had there been a lot of black smoke or black buildings in the top left of the picture, white lettering would have been in order. But the light area dictates the use of black letters, and to express this particular idea, too, black would be the better choice.

Here is a contrast. Now what would you do? Obviously the lettering must be light in weight. Should we use a Gill Sans or perhaps a script? The artist has left an area above the shoe which is light. Should we put a dark band at the top of the picture and put a light letter over it? That would keep the shoe and its name the same. Well, there is no one answer—you do it.

60

LETTERING AND THE ART SCHOOL

In this day and age, more and more commercial enterprises and industries are springing up. This means more advertising—and more work for graphic artists and typographers. The standard is high, but the standard of training in art schools is also high. Whether you, as a Young Letterer, go on to study at a school depends on whether you want to make a living from lettering or whether you are interested in it only as a hobby.

Even if it is only a hobby, many people of all ages go to art school for professional tuition, which can be obtained by studying either part time or full time. You will find that as your interest in lettering develops, you will be comparing and criticizing the great many styles that are to be seen around you. In this age of advertising there is no lack of lettering, whether it be type-set, drawn, or incised. Look out for, and study the examples of lettering on shop fronts, displays, posters, road signs, letterheads—in fact everywhere that lettering is to be found.

For the serious student with his career ahead of him, several years at art school will be spent on many art subjects which will include calligraphy, drawn lettering, graphic art and typography.

When I was an art student, there seemed to be a 'great divide' between students of typography and those studying drawn lettering. This is not only a pity, it is stupid. I'm glad to say both sides nowadays realize that there is much to learn from the other. Indeed, whether you lay out and set up type, or whether you lay out and draw the letters, the important fact is that you are preparing something of good design that is to be read!

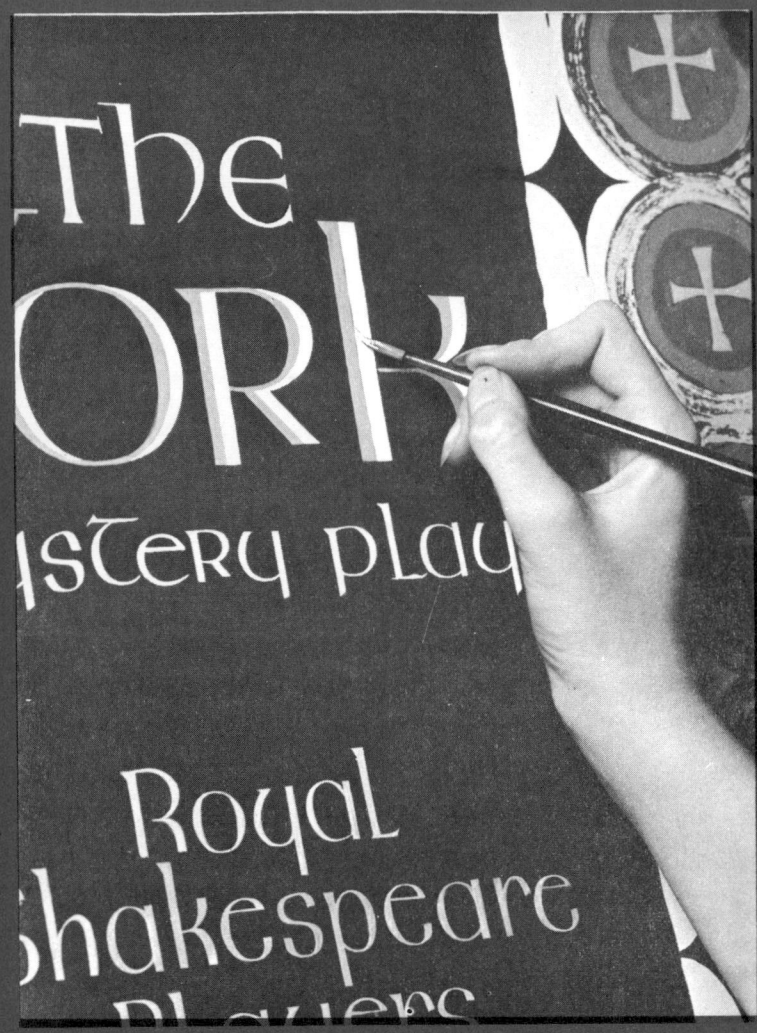

Drawn lettering by Miss Joan Mathews,
Epsom and Ewell School of Art

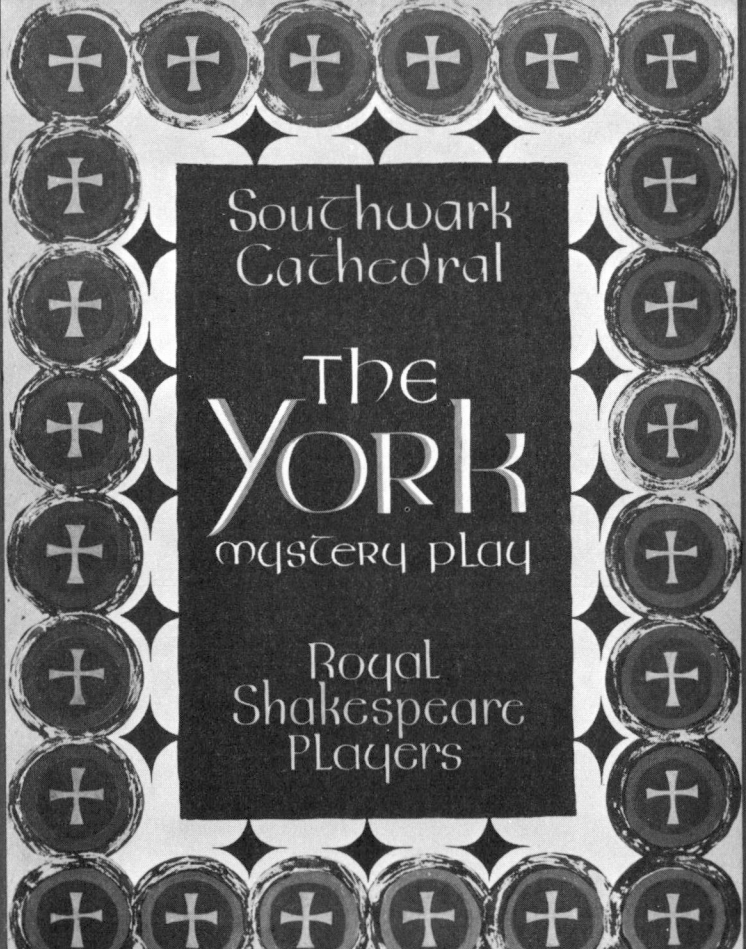

How Lettering Can be Used

The uses to which you will put your knowledge of lettering will, naturally, be determined by your study and experience of the subject. I think it well that you should know what sort of work is available to a good graphic artist who has specialized in lettering. Large firms in every branch of industry need to advertise themselves. This may be by means of the printed word in the form of a brochure—which has to be laid out, the type chosen, the lettering drawn. The firm may have packaging problems—here again the lettering artist is needed. The smallest shop has to put sales tickets on its goods: they have to be drawn by someone. Advertising agencies employ lettering and graphic artists. You would be expected to take along some examples of your work to show if you hoped to work in a commercial studio of this sort. Exhibitions are constantly being held and think of the various lettering jobs needed in this connection. Then, apart from the highly professional work that is done in vast quantities for the world of commerce, there are many pleasing jobs to be done for local councils and organizations. Museums and libraries often use the talents of local students. I have seen beautiful lettering on their notices and displays in many places.

Television, too, is employing more graphic artists. Lettering on television—as for anything else—has to be carefully chosen to give the best result for the particular medium.

It is certainly rewarding to know that art schools and colleges in Britain and America and on the Continent are keeping up the craft of calligraphy and that beautiful examples can be seen everywhere. In recent years, the wish to write well has come to people outside art schools and the calligrapher's spade nib has worked its way over many an ordinary letter and envelope.

So whether your knowledge of lettering allows you to design the name of a vast corporation of international repute, or whether it allows you to write a satisfactorily legible postcard, the result will be the same —good lettering that will not only satisfy you, but will help to bring about more and more good design in a world that has for thousands of years, and will until the end of time, use this fascinating craft of lettering.

Other Books on Lettering

THE ART OF HAND-LETTERING
    by Helm Wotzkow
    Watson-Guptill Publications Inc., New York (Now out of print)

THE CRAFT OF LETTERING
    by John R. Biggs
    Pitman Publishing Corp., New York

THE CRAFT OF THE PEN
    by John R. Biggs
    Pitman Publishing Corp., New York

THE 'PUFFIN' BOOK OF LETTERING
    by Tom Gourdie
    Penguin Books, Baltimore, Maryland

MONOTYPE COMPOSITION FACES
    Lanston Monotype Co, New York

MONOTYPE DISPLAY FACES
    Lanston Monotype Co, New York

26 LETTERS
    by Oscar Ogg
    Thomas Y. Crowell Co, New York

Acknowledgements

This book has taken me, on and off, three years to put together. It is something I have wanted to do for a very long time. Now it is done. It could not have been done without the help and advice of other people. Everyone I've been in contact with over the book has been enthusiastic. I do thank them all very much.

Especially glad was I to have the expert help and advice of Mrs Beatrice Warde, B.A., who has taken a more than friendly interest.

I am grateful:

    to Mr Robert A. Strand, A.R.C.A., A.T.D., Principal of the Epsom and Ewell School of Art, for his interest and help;

    to his Graphic Design Department and Lecturer in Charge: Mr B. Gordon Smith, M.S.I.A., and the Staff and Students;

    to the Keeper of the Library, Victoria and Albert Museum;

    to the Vice-Provost and Librarian, Trinity College, Dublin;

    to Urs Graf Verlag, Olten, Switzerland;

    to the Monotype Corporation Ltd, who have kindly provided the specimens on pages 50 to 58;

    to my wife for typing it all and correcting the spelling.

But above all I am grateful to the Principal and Staff of Maidstone College of Art of some eighteen years back. They never suspected I had become so interested in Lettering.